Human Body Systems

The Digestive System

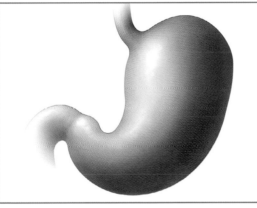

by Rebecca Olien

Consultant:
Marjorie Hogan, MD
Pediatrician
Hennepin County Medical Center
Minneapolis, Minnesota

Capstone
press

Mankato, Minnesota

Bridgestone Books are published by Capstone Press,
151 Good Counsel Drive, P.O. Box 669, Mankato, Minnesota 56002.
www.capstonepress.com

Library of Congress Cataloging-in-Publication Data
Olien, Rebecca.
   The digestive system / by Rebecca Olien.
      p. cm.—(Bridgestone books. Human body systems)
   Summary: "Learn about the job of the digestive system, problems that may arise, and how to keep
the system healthy"—Provided by publisher.
   Includes bibliographical references and index.
   ISBN-13: 978-0-7368-5409-2 (hardcover)
   ISBN-10: 0-7368-5409-6 (hardcover)
   1. Digestive organs—Juvenile literature. I. Title. II. Bridgestone Books. Human body systems.
QP145O54 2006
612.3—dc22   2005021147

Editorial Credits
Amber Bannerman, editor; Bobbi J. Dey, designer; Kelly Garvin, photo researcher/photo editor

Photo Credits
BananaStock, Ltd., 8
Capstone Press/Karon Dubke, cover (boy), 4, 18, 20
Getty Images Inc./David Trood Pictures, 6
Photo Researchers Inc./Anatomical Travelogue, 10; BSIP/VERO/CARLO, cover (intestines); David
    Gifford, 16; John M. Daugherty, 1; Medical Art Service, 14; Professor Peter Cull, 12
Visuals Unlimited/Dr. Kessel & Dr. Kardon/Tissues & Organs, 16 (inset)

1 2 3 4 5 6 11 10 09 08 07 06

Table of Contents

4

Food on the Move

Crunch! Take a big bite of stringy celery. As you chew, the celery has already started its journey through the digestive system. Everything you eat travels 30 feet (9 meters) through your digestive tract.

The digestive system is just one of your body's systems. It helps the body use food. Other body systems help you breathe, pump blood, and think. All of them work together to keep you going.

◄ Celery is a healthy snack.

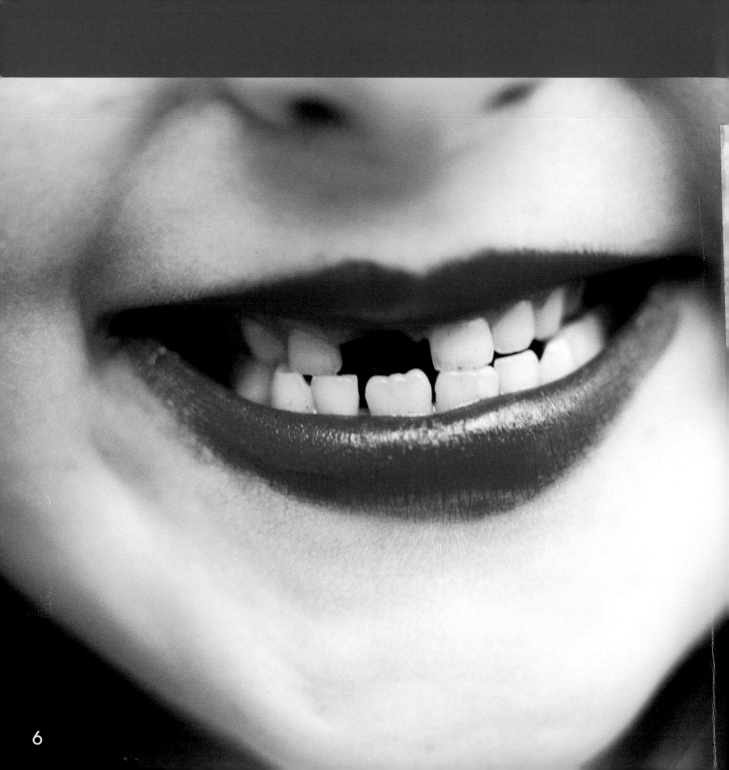

Getting Nutrients

Digestion starts with your teeth and ends when waste leaves your body. Your body breaks down food during digestion. During this process, your body takes in **nutrients** that are found in what you eat and drink.

Your body needs nutrients to stay healthy. Water, carbohydrates, fats, protein, minerals, and vitamins are the main nutrients. They give your body energy. Energy helps you run, talk, think, breathe, and grow.

◄ Your strong teeth help you chew food, beginning the digestion process.

The Mouth

Digestion begins with the mouth. Your front teeth take a big bite of a juicy apple. Back molar teeth grind the apple into smaller pieces. **Saliva** in the mouth makes the bite of apple soft and wet.

When it becomes mushy, the apple is ready to be swallowed. The tongue rolls the soft, chewed apple into a ball. The ball of food is easy to swallow.

◄ Your teeth and saliva help turn a bite of a hard apple into a mushy ball you can swallow.

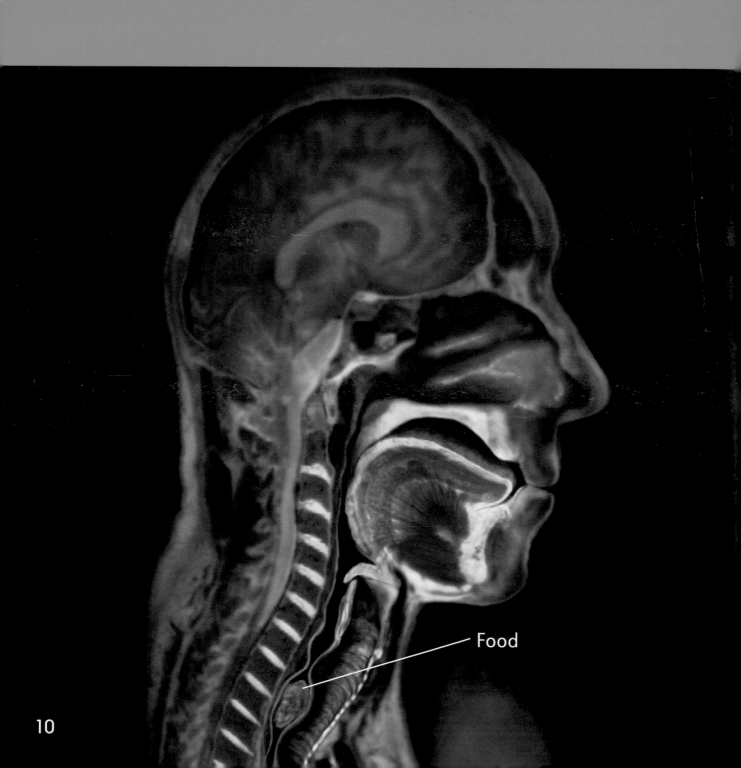

Food

The Upper Digestive Tract

Swallowed food travels into the upper digestive tract. The upper digestive tract includes the throat, **esophagus**, and stomach. Swallowing pushes food down the throat into the tube-shaped esophagus.

Food travels 10 inches (25 centimeters) down the esophagus. Muscles around the esophagus move food the way fingers squeeze toothpaste from a tube. At the end of the esophagus, a ring of muscle controls how much food enters the stomach.

◄ A chewed ball of food moves through the esophagus on its way to the stomach.

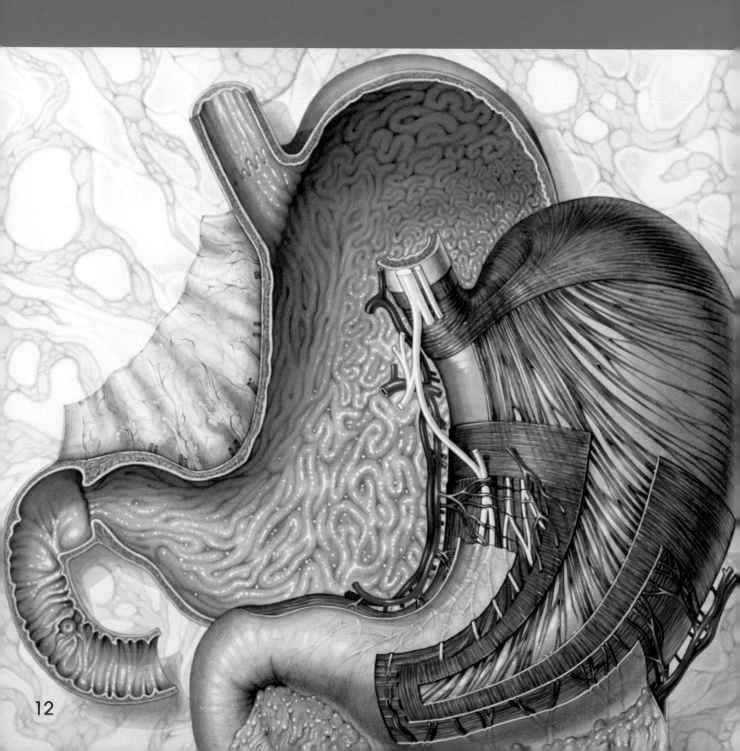

The Stomach

The stomach is a hollow pouch where food collects. As it fills with food, the stomach stretches like a balloon. Food stays in the stomach about 3 hours.

During this time, food is mixed and churned by the stomach's powerful muscles. The stomach adds **acid** and other liquids to the food. These liquids help break down food into a soupy mixture. They also kill many germs found in food. A slimy layer of **mucus** protects stomach walls from the strong acid.

◀ A cut view of a stomach shows both the inside (left) and outside (right).

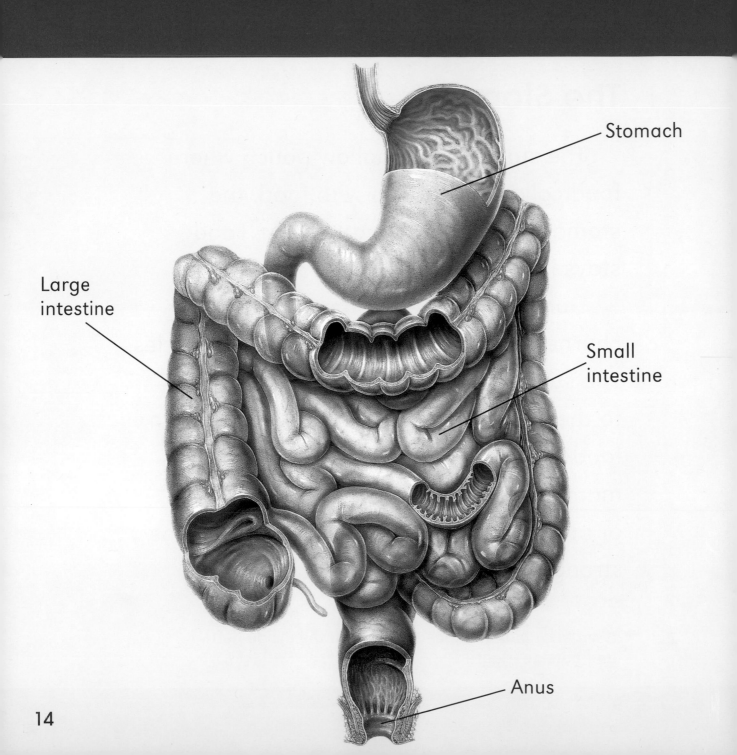

Stomach

Large
intestine

Small
intestine

Anus

The Lower Digestive Tract

The small intestine is the longest part of the digestive system. If straightened, it would stretch 22 feet (6.7 meters). The small intestine is coiled under the stomach. Nutrients are absorbed into the bloodstream from the small intestine.

The parts of food the body can't use travel into the large intestine. The large intestine is shorter and wider than the small intestine. The large intestine absorbs water and stores waste. The body gets rid of the waste at the anus as stool when you go to the bathroom.

◄ The stomach, small intestine, large intestine, and anus are all important parts of the digestive system.

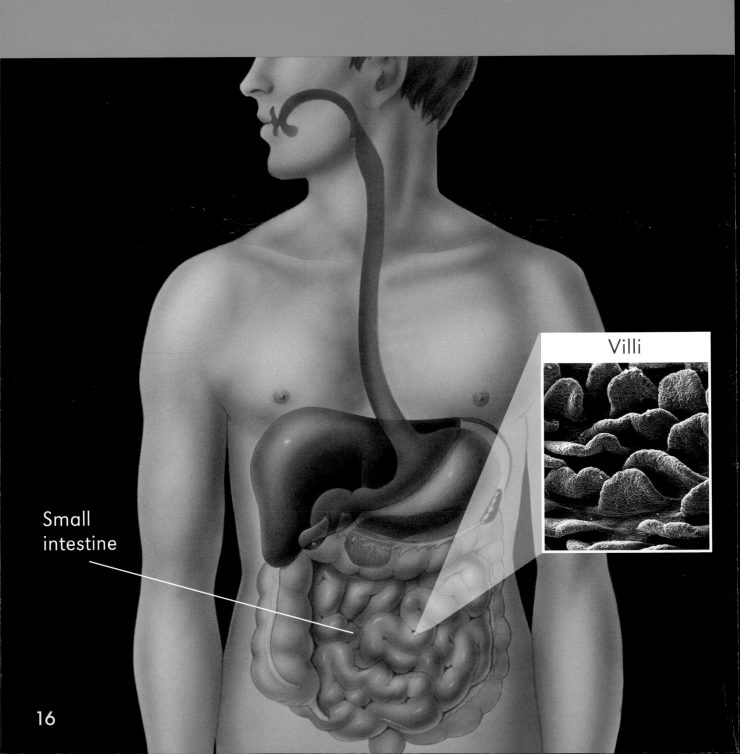

Villi

Small
intestine

Digestion and Circulation

Nutrients stay in the small intestine for a short while. The pancreas, liver, and gallbladder send juices into the small intestine. These juices help break down nutrients found in food.

The circulatory system and digestive system work together to pass along nutrients. Millions of tongue-shaped **villi** soak up nutrients in the small intestine. Tiny blood vessels meet the villi and pick up the nutrients. Blood carries the nutrients through the circulatory system to the rest of the body.

◀ The small photo shows a close-up view of villi.

Digestive Problems

Problems with the digestive system are common. Germs can cause stomachaches. People with the stomach flu can spread their germs. Germs from spoiled food can also make people sick.

Your body gets rid of germs and bad food by throwing up or having diarrhea. Throwing up causes food to leave the stomach, travel up the esophagus, and go out of the mouth. Diarrhea happens when germs travel quickly through the intestines. Water is not soaked up, so stool is watery.

◀ Most stomachaches are caused by germs.

Healthy Habits

Getting rid of germs will keep your digestive system healthy. Wash fruits and vegetables before eating them. Scrub your hands with soap and water often to wash away germs. Cooking meats properly also kills germs.

Your body needs a variety of foods to stay healthy. Fruits and vegetables give the body vitamins and minerals. Beans, nuts, meat, and eggs give the body protein. Breads and cereals provide carbohydrates for energy. Foods with fiber keep food moving through the digestive tract. Make healthy eating a habit for life.

◄ Washing vegetables gets rid of dirt and germs.

Glossary

acid (ASS-id)—a substance in the stomach that breaks down food for the body to use

esophagus (e-SOF-uh-guhss)—the tube that carries food from the mouth to the stomach; muscles in the esophagus push food into the stomach.

mucus (MYOO-kuhss)—a slimy, thick liquid

nutrient (NOO-tree-uhnt)—something that is needed by people, animals, and plants to stay healthy and strong

saliva (suh-LYE-vuh)—the clear liquid in your mouth that helps you swallow and begin to digest food

villi (VIH-lye)—tiny parts of the small intestine that soak up nutrients

Read More

Parker, Steve. *Digestion.* Our Bodies. Chicago: Raintree, 2004.

Rau, Dana Meachen. *My Stomach.* Bookworms. What's Inside Me? Tarrytown, N.Y.: Marshall Cavendish, 2005.

Internet Sites

FactHound offers a safe, fun way to find Internet sites related to this book. All of the sites on FactHound have been researched by our staff.

Here's how:

1. Visit *www.facthound.com*
2. Type in this special code **0736854096** for age-appropriate sites. Or enter a search word related to this book for a more general search.
3. Click on the **Fetch It** button.

FactHound will fetch the best sites for you!

Index